FIRST FAMILIES

An Intimate Portrait
from the Kennedys
to the Clintons

HARRY BENSON

with forewords by
Rosalynn Carter, Nancy Reagan,
and Barbara Bush

edited by
Gigi Benson and David Friend

A Bulfinch Press Book
Little, Brown and Company
Boston New York Toronto London

I would like to thank David Friend, Jonathan Delano,
Carol Leslie, Dorothy Williams, Kay Douglas, Tom Voss,
M. C. Marden, John Loengard, and Benjamina Baron
for their invaluable help in getting this book published.
I would like to dedicate *First Families* to my wife, Gigi,
and my daughters, Wendy and Tessa.

Photographs and text copyright © 1997 by Harry Benson Ltd.
Foreword by Rosalynn Carter copyright © 1997 by Rosalynn Carter
Foreword by Nancy Reagan copyright © 1997 by Nancy Reagan
Foreword by Barbara Bush copyright © 1997 by Barbara Bush

First edition

FRONTISPIECE: The Clintons playing cards, 1992.

Design by Douglas + Voss

Library of Congress Cataloging-in-Publication Data
Benson, Harry.
        First families: an intimate portrait from the Kennedys to the Clintons / Harry
    Benson. — 1st ed.
            p. cm.
        ISBN 0-8212-2360-7
            1. Presidents—United States—Family—History—20th century—Miscellanea.
        2. Presidents—United States—Family—Pictorial works.
        I. Title.
        E176.1.B445 1997
        973.92'092'2—dc21
        [B]
                                                                                                    97-1418

Bulfinch Press is an imprint and trademark of
Little, Brown and Company (Inc.)
Published simultaneously in Canada by
Little, Brown & Company (Canada) Limited

PRINTED IN THE UNITED STATES OF AMERICA

CONTENTS

In 1961 I was working for a London newspaper and was assigned to follow President and Mrs. Kennedy around London and Paris. It's hard to believe that that was thirty-five years ago, and that I've had the opportunity to photograph every U.S. president since. Some presidents I've photographed closely, over and over again, others not as often as I would have liked.

David Friend, Director of Photography and New Media for *Life*, has been saying for a long time that he thought I had a book in these presidential photos. He once asked me how many presidents I had photographed. I answered, "Every one since Kennedy," then I stopped and said, "No, that's not right. I did photograph Eisenhower once in the 1950s after he had finished a round of golf in Turnberry, Scotland." It was a picture I was very proud of — his glasses at the end of his nose, he looked aghast at his score. The picture is lost. At the time I was working for the *Hamilton Advertiser,* the largest weekly newspaper in Scotland.

When I photographed President and Mrs. Kennedy in London in 1961 it was from a newsman's perspective, when they were on the streets, out in public. I thought if only I could get inside, I could really show something about their lives. The trouble with photo ops is that people put on their public faces to be photographed. There is a large corps of White House writers and photographers who follow a president's every move. That presents a problem as to how to get something different, something exclusive. My main challenge is to take a photograph that shows an intimacy, not something the press secretary thought up. To me this has always been the hardest part. I want to show the families candidly, in a friendly, human way. I like to keep my photographs moving, keep them light and quick. I want to show a freedom in my pictures, not have them stiff, formal, and posed. Photographing a president is for the history books; it's for the archives.

When I photographed Presidents Kennedy and Johnson, I was working as a freelancer for a Fleet Street newspaper, which has not the same influence as say a *Life* magazine has. My first visit to the White House was to photograph Lyndon Johnson signing a bill. He had a big bunch of pens on his desk beside him. He would sign the *L* with one pen, the *Y* with another, the *N* with another, and give each pen to some dignitary standing nearby. When he got to the *H* in *Johnson,* he held out the pen and beckoned to me. I thought the president was calling the photographer next to me, who nudged me and said, "He's calling you, go on up there." The president handed me the pen and kept his hand out for me to shake as I thanked him. I was so taken with myself that I walked out of the White House, past the security gate, and didn't hand in my White House pass. I wanted to keep it as a souvenir as well. The White House police called within an hour saying I had not turned in my pass and they wanted it back. I dropped it off before returning to New York that night.

I remember one day some time later going up to the securi-

With my daughter Tessa and Mrs. Clinton on the Truman Balcony, 1993.

INTRODUCTION

ty box outside the White House and casually flipping out what I thought was my green *Life* press pass to show the guards at the gate. I started to walk right on in when one of them said, "I don't want to offend you, Mr. Benson, but do you have any other credentials?" I said, "What could be better than *Life* magazine?" and then I looked down and saw that I had mistakenly handed the guard a green charge card from the Fin 'N Claw fish restaurant on Lexington Avenue in New York. I was embarrassed and not quite as nonchalant as before. I said, "Yes, I've got a better one than that," and we all had a laugh.

I am not under any illusions. It is the magazine I carry in my back pocket that carries the weight, that determines whether a president will agree to take time out to be photographed, and it is up to me to deliver the photographs once I get there. Being a photographer I'm looking at the subject's eyes all the time — looking for boredom to set in. I'm watching very closely. That is why I work very quickly. I never do a Polaroid after the president comes into the room. He is too busy to wait for me to check the lighting, and it is degrading for a head of state to stand posing for too long. I time every picture I do. I can see the situation. I never take my eyes off him, for if I do he's gone, literally. He's lost his concentration, and I'll never get him back.

When you watch a president from the beginning of his term of office to the end, you can see his administration changing, becoming more streamlined, more professional. In the beginning the people who arrange access to the president are obliging — the president and the family are readily accessible. Later on they are less so, but it is not just the access, it's more specifically a question of what they will do for you. It's only natural that people will change. It's noticeable in their clothes, their hair. As time goes on, the president becomes more presidential, the suits become made-to-measure, the neckties become more tasteful, and the man becomes more statesmanlike. The pressure of the office begins to show on his face, too. At the beginning of a campaign or a term of office you grab the moment and take as much as you can get, photographically speaking, because later on invariably it will change.

If I wanted to know the mood of the White House on a certain day, I would look at the secret servicemen, the press aides, and the secretaries. Their faces would tell me what to expect. When I've been given an assignment to photograph a president in the White House or wherever, my editor will tell me, "You'll have an hour." I know I'll be lucky to get ten minutes. My philosophy is that speed isn't everything, it's the only thing. Which also means that technically correct photography can go out the window. I've never said that's what magazines are about. They're about what is happening at that moment, catching a moment — they're about photojournalism. While I'm in the White House press room waiting to go in to photograph the president, I know someone is going to come into the room and say, "We've scheduled a half hour for you." A little later he'll come back and say, "You couldn't have picked a worse morning. All

With Jonathan Delano at Caroline Kennedy's wedding to Edwin Schlossberg, 1986.

Photographing Mrs. Carter in the Blue Room, 1979.

Photographing President and Mrs. Clinton with Jonathan Delano in the White House, 1993.

With President Nixon in the Rose Garden, 1971.

With President and Mrs. Reagan in the White House, 1985.

No book would be complete without a photograph of my family: wife, Gigi, center, with daughters Wendy, left, and Tessa, 1996.

we've got is fifteen minutes." Then, "This may have to be rescheduled." All this is off-putting and tension mounts. It always happens. Finally I get ten minutes, and I am ready for them.

I was never in the White House pool or the personal photographer to a president, but rather from time to time I documented each of the eight presidents from Kennedy to Clinton. This is a personal memoir, a personal journey of the past thirty-five years. It is my look at the first families. Looking at the photographs, I have realized how each family brought their own distinct personality, their own style to the White House, to Pennsylvania Avenue. I am thankful to all the first ladies. While all the other photographers were clamoring to get in the front door of the White House, using the same crowded press conference route, I tried to concentrate on the wives and families and was busy going through the side door. And it almost always worked.

Three first ladies were kind enough to write a reminiscence of their time in the White House for my book and I am most appreciative of their taking the time to do so. I have always been aware of the importance of the first lady. It's obvious she has the ear of the president, and it's interesting to see how these three, Mrs. Carter, Mrs. Reagan, and Mrs. Bush, have remembered their time in the White House.

Capture is an overused word, but I have tried to capture some intimate moments in the life of each of the presidents I've had the opportunity to photograph. I'm lucky to have been put in the unique position of documenting the lives of eight first families. When you are put in that position, you just have to try to come through it the best way you can.

Dear Harry,

The Truman balcony was my favorite place in the White House. The view is the most beautiful in all of Washington. Looking out over the south lawn we could see the Ellipse across the street, the Washington monument and the Jefferson memorial. Jimmy and I spent many late afternoons or evenings after dinner sitting there, talking about what had happened during the day. It was private and peaceful — a wonderful retreat

Sincerely,

Rosalynn Carter

OFFICE OF NANCY REAGAN

August 26, 1996

Dear Mr. Benson:

The White House is a magical place for Americans. It symbolizes so much of our history as a nation and the world's perception of where the mantle of leadership is housed. But what is so special, and so uniquely American, is that this imposing, white columned fortress is really just a home, where family and friends roam through the halls and breakfast is served after a night's rest (although sometimes not too much rest).

For all this history, protocol and genuine eloquence that this stately old mansion exudes, it truly was for us, our home. Ronnie still likes to say that we lived above the store, and I think that attitude is a reflection of his greatness -- he always knew that we were just given temporary use today and that the American people were gracious enough to let us stay there two full terms. I hope they feel that we were good stewards of our time there. We tried to do our best.

Those eight years were not always easy and included many days when the sun did not look like it would shine, but our hearts for each other were housed there during that perod in our lives and every crisis, whether national or personal, became a little easier to deal with.

Ron and I will never forget our years at the White House. We often think of our friends there and stay in touch with them. After eight years you really do become a family.

From the both of us, we thank each every one of you who made it possible. May God bless you. May God grant wisdom and grace to each family who occupies the White House. And may God bless our United States of America.

Sincerely,

Nancy Reagan

Barbara Bush

From the very beginning, we knew living in the White House would be a whole new experience. At our very first family dinner, we noticed two 7-year-old grandchildren missing. One of the White House butlers told us they had ordered hamburgers to be served to them in the White House bowling alley. Their dreams of a grand lifestyle quickly ended when they were ordered upstairs to eat dinner with the family and informed there would be no special-orders.

It may surprise you to learn the White House was a great place for our family to gather. One Sunday afternoon we were having a particularly relaxing family day. George was playing horseshoes nearby while I swam laps in the pool. I had just gotten started when a great big rat swam right in front of my mask. I flew out of the pool screaming. The Secret Service couldn't decide what to do about it. George calmly walked over and drowned the nasty little creature.

Christmas was particularly a special time for us, starting with the 40 volunteers who came every year to turn the White House into a winter wonderland, to the musicians and chefs, to the 12 grandchildren arriving from all over the country to enjoy it all. It was a glorious time of faith, family, and friends.

Of course the responsibility weighing on George was tremendous. The pressure was always there, but never felt more deeply than when he had to send troops into combat. George worked late into many nights and often had to be awakened hours before dawn about one crisis or another.

Nevertheless, we loved living in the White House. After all, there were 93 wonderful household staff whose only concern was making us happy. They were like family. And I probably saw more of George then than in any other time of our marriage. After all, we lived "above the store."

We'll always feel grateful to the American people for giving us the great privilege of calling the White House home.

Barbara Bush

PRESIDENTS

JOHN FITZGERALD KENNEDY
35TH PRESIDENT OF THE UNITED STATES (1961–1963)
*Born May 29, 1917,
in Brookline, Massachusetts
Married Jacqueline Lee Bouvier, 1953*

It was starting to rain that day in the summer of 1961. President Kennedy was to lay a wreath on the grave of the unknown soldier at the Arc de Triomphe in Paris. I arrived just as the president did so it was difficult to get a position in the crowd. There was a narrow, five-foot-high ledge near the Arc. I had my camera bag slung over my shoulder and I climbed up on the stone wall which was getting slippery in the rain. President Kennedy watched me struggling up the ledge trying to quickly change film — he actually observed me for almost half a minute with a kind look, as if to say, "It's okay, take your time," as if he was sympathetic to a young photographer's desperation to get an important picture. There was a steady drizzle by now and someone offered him an umbrella. He politely pushed it away with his hand. There was no way he was going to be photographed with an umbrella, an object that had the connotation of Neville Chamberlain and the appeasement of Hitler at Munich before World War II broke out. You can see the rain on his shoulders and his steady, knowing gaze.

LYNDON BAINES JOHNSON
36TH PRESIDENT OF THE UNITED STATES (1963–1969)
*Born August 27, 1908, in Stonewall, Texas
Married Claudia Alta "Lady Bird" Taylor, 1934*

President Johnson was the most distinguished-looking president I have encountered, a tough yet decent man. He had deep, piercing eyes. When I photograph someone I always look at his eyes. And each of the presidents I've met has had a common trait: an awareness of his surroundings and an ability to take in everything in the room at once, which are signs of perception, intensity, and power. And no one more so than Johnson. This photograph was taken in the Oval Office in 1966 during one of my first White House visits. When I told the president that my fiancée's father was a fellow Texan, his eyes twinkled.

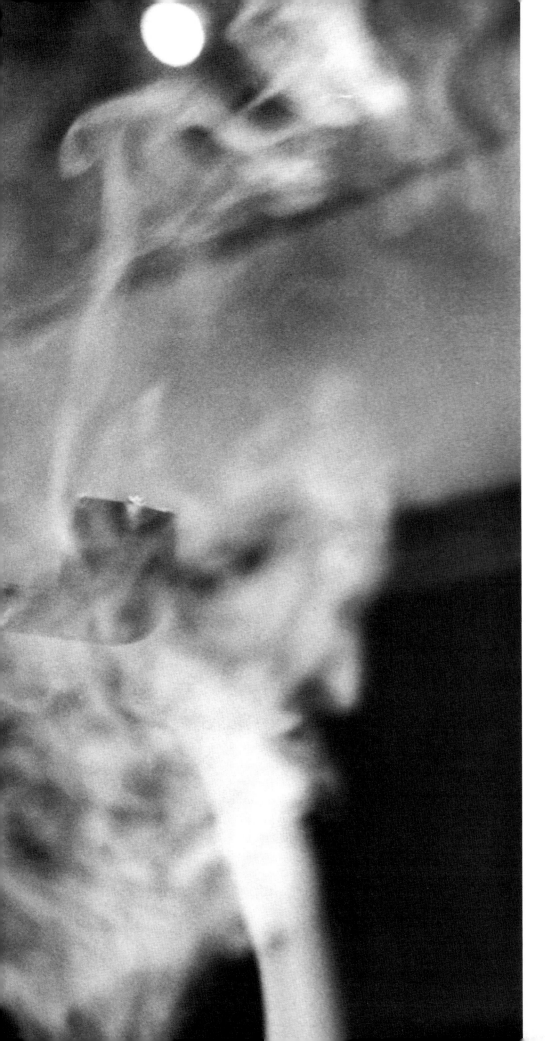

GERALD RUDOLPH FORD
38TH PRESIDENT OF THE
UNITED STATES (1974–1977)
Born July 14, 1913, in Omaha, Nebraska
Married Elizabeth "Betty" Bloomer Warren, 1948

A very amiable, respectful man, Ford was easygoing yet he was a man who projected considerable stature as well, having been the House minority leader when President Nixon selected him to be his vice president in 1973. I was photographing him in his new plane — Air Force Two, I believe — just after he had been appointed vice president. He took a moment, during the flight from Boston to Washington, D.C., to sit with me and talk awhile, casual and open despite the formality of his tuxedo, the pipe smoke curling up around him.

James Earl Carter
39th President of the
United States (1977–1981)
Born October 1, 1924, in Plains, Georgia
Married Rosalynn Smith, 1946

When I photographed President Carter in
the Oval Office in late 1979, I asked him if
he ever looked out the window to get a
glimpse of the world beyond. He said,
"Whenever I've got a moment. Actually, I've
done it a lot these days." And so I asked him
to peer out as I went outside, looking back
in. At the time, the U.S. embassy staff was
being held hostage in Iran and the tension of
the crisis showed on his face. The glass between us felt like a wall, as if I weren't even
there. To me, this picture shows the loneli-
ness and isolation of every man who inhabits
the Oval Office.

RONALD WILSON REAGAN
40TH PRESIDENT OF THE UNITED STATES (1981–1989)
Born February 6, 1911, in Tampico, Illinois
Married Anne Frances "Nancy" Robbins Davis, 1952

The first time I photographed Ronald Reagan was at his California ranch in November 1966, just before he was elected governor. This photograph was taken for *Life* on the terrace of his West Coast office, in Century City, twenty-one years later, near the end of his presidency. Down below him you can see the 20th Century Fox film studio. He pointed to a soundstage where he had worked early in his Hollywood career. He learned how to project his image there. The world came to know him as the Great Communicator, and that he was. He could command your attention when he spoke. And when he told a joke or an amusing anecdote about an actor, director, or another politician, you didn't have to pretend to laugh. You would really laugh. He was one of the few people I've met who I can say was a compelling storyteller.

GEORGE HERBERT WALKER BUSH
41ST PRESIDENT OF THE
UNITED STATES (1989–1993)
Born June 12, 1924, in Milton, Massachusetts
Married Barbara Pierce, 1945

In December 1986, George Bush, who was vice president at the time, was leaving his office in the White House on his way to the Capitol Building. He invited me to join him in his limousine: "Hi, Harry. Just jump in the car with me. I'm going over to the Capitol." It was friendly, relaxed — he was comfortable to be with. Though he asked me to sit in the seat beside him, I said that I'd rather sit in the jump seat across in order to have a better position from which to photograph him. He was the most unassuming president. And his Secret Service agents also seemed the nicest. Instead of scowling, they smiled — and kept out of my way when I was busy with their boss. The White House photographers I knew said Bush was a nice guy who genuinely liked photographers.

WILLIAM JEFFERSON CLINTON
42ND PRESIDENT OF THE
UNITED STATES (1993–   )
Born August 19, 1946, in Hope, Arkansas
Married Hillary Rodham, 1975

President Clinton had been a Rhodes Scholar at Oxford. Noticing my accent the first time I photographed him, he said, "From Scotland?" I answered, "Glasgow." He went on to say, "I've been to Kirkcudbright," which he pronounced correctly — Kir-Koo-Bree. It was a county in southern Scotland. I complimented his correct pronunciation, saying, "You're the only American I've ever met who could say it properly." He told me he used to go up there when he was an Oxford student and insisted he'd return to visit some day. This portrait was taken in Little Rock in June 1992, and I reminded him of the first time we'd met, some months before, during the New Hampshire primary campaign, when I'd asked his motorcade to stop so I could take his picture beside a similar tree. It had been a cold, bleak day and I was about to take the photograph that would be his first cover story of the race, for *New York* magazine. Now he reminds me of that photograph each time we meet.

FIRST
LADIES

Previous spread:

Mrs. Kennedy was visiting her sister, Princess Lee Radziwill, at her home near Buckingham Palace in 1961 and she came out to give the waiting photographers a picture.

Many years later when Mrs. Kennedy telephoned to ask me to photograph Caroline's wedding in 1986, she was so very soft spoken that I thought it was someone playing a prank. I asked her where she had lunch the day before; coincidentally, I had been in the same restaurant. She answered, "Mortimer's. Second table on the right."

And I said, "Yes, Mrs. Kennedy, may I help you?"

Although her name by that time was Mrs. Onassis, the few times I spoke with her I found it difficult to call her anything but Mrs. Kennedy. This is how I remember her, as the elegant first lady I photographed in Paris and London in 1961.

Set in the Texas Hill Country, the LBJ ranch was impressive. And I had a knowledgeable tour guide, Lady Bird Johnson, who showed me around, inside and out. I was doing a story for *Life* on former first ladies and, upon meeting her, I got the impression that she missed President Johnson deeply, always coming back to memories of "Lyndon." The whole day was quite melancholy in that respect. By then — September of 1985 — Mrs. Johnson had achieved some renown for her program to beautify America by planting trees, and at one point she sat beside a beautiful live oak. She told me that she had wanted to plant one at the White House but the live oak would not grow well that far north.

In May 1974, first lady Pat Nixon graciously welcomed a Republican women's delegation to the White House. To me, the most surprising thing about her was her deep voice. Tall and lithe, the perfect hostess, she had a knack for spotting every little detail as events swirled around her. Over the years, several White House staff members have told me that in retrospect Mrs. Nixon was their favorite first lady. Some of them had even been there since FDR's time. They told me she never forgot a birthday and always inquired when someone was ill. Some tell me they still miss her. I've probably got a soft spot for her, for when my first daughter, Wendy, was born, Mrs. Nixon sent her a lovely pink dress.

I photographed Elizabeth "Betty" Ford for *Vogue* outside her home in Alexandria, Virginia, in 1974. At the time her husband was still the vice president. Having read that she was once a model, I asked her to recline in the grass to show off her dress. She was a good sport and it was an opportunity for her to be a model again. I think she handled it well. A surprisingly sensitive woman, yet outspoken and forthright, she faced her challenges openly and is proud of the help that her Betty Ford Center has given to countless people battling their dependencies.

Rosalynn Carter was utterly unassuming. Everything I asked of her during any photography session, she would oblige. She never said, "I don't think I'd look good in that pose" or anything like that. She was receptive, very honest, and straightforward. And during this particular shoot in Plains, Georgia, in January of 1986, I remember thinking she was really quite beautiful. I never got the sense that she was looking at her watch or trying to catch an assistant's eye to hurry things along. Flying back to New York, I always found myself thinking that I could have done more. In fact, there was something very open about the whole Carter family. When I spoke with them, there were no airs or graces, which is not to say that they were not well mannered. They answered any question put to them, which I found refreshing.

Previous spread:
Nancy Reagan greeted me in her dressing gown at the door of
her Bel Air, California, home for a 1995 *Vanity Fair* photo. Her
hair and makeup were perfect — she was all ready to go, as she
was every time I've photographed her. There was never any waiting, no sitting around wondering when — or if — she was
going to emerge. That day she showed me two dresses and asked
which I preferred. She loved red, of course. Pointing to a red
Galanos, I said, "I like that one," and she said, "So do I." I got
the feeling she really enjoyed these sessions. "Where do you
want me, Harry? That's fine." For this photograph, we were not
in the main library of the house but in a smaller one. I saw a
needlepoint cushion lying on the sofa with the initials *R.R.* on
it. I had to show that. The president, she told me, had been out
playing golf the day before. And then her dog, Rex, jumped up
on the couch as well. I found her one of the most thoughtful of
all the first ladies, actually. She really made sure that no one
around her was ever being overlooked. And she was ever mind-
ful of her husband's legacy, hoping people would remember him
as "the Great Communicator." The Reagans were really quite
close; you could feel a warmth between them as you could with
the Carters.

That Barbara Bush was the daughter of magazine publisher
Marvin Pierce was a fact I did not know when I first photographed her. It may have contributed to her astuteness in deal-
ing with the press. Her fine-tuned sense of humor didn't hurt
either. By the time the Bushes had arrived in the White House,
their children were grown and the world-famous Millie, a King
Charles spaniel, went everywhere the first lady went. Millie had
been a present from the president after her old cocker spaniel,
C. Fred, had died in 1987. The First Dog, of course, went on to
publish *Millie's Book,* ghostwritten by Mrs. Bush, a champion of
children's literature. For this 1989 *Good Housekeeping* photograph, Mrs. Bush wore a Scaasi gown as she finalized prepara-
tions for a White House state dinner that evening.

Left: Congressman Gerald Ford's nomination for vice president had just been approved by the Senate when I photographed him at his home outside Washington, D.C., in 1973. He liked to get up early, before the rest of his family awoke. He would fix breakfast, read the papers in solitude, and then wash his own dishes.

Above: This Ford family portrait was taken at their Alexandria, Virginia, home in January of 1974. Steve, seventeen, and Susan, sixteen, are pictured; sons Michael and Jack were away at college at the time.

Previous spread: In June 1992, I flew down to the governor's mansion in Little Rock, Arkansas, to photograph the Clinton family for *People.* The governor was the front runner in the race for the presidency. I was looking for something to use as a prop to make the pictures informal — even cozy — when I spotted the hammock in the backyard. The Clintons were excited about the prospect of moving to Washington, and you can see from their faces how close they seemed as a family.

Left: As soon as Gerald Ford was named vice president in 1973, their quiet neighborhood in Alexandria, Virginia, was transformed. All of a sudden the Secret Service had placed a sentry post in their backyard. The photograph, of son Steve, a high school senior, inspecting a motorcycle with his now-famous dad, was taken outside their home.

Above, top: Susan Ford sat beside the family swimming pool at their Virginia home in June 1974.

Above: Jack Ford relaxed on his Hobie Cat in Mission Bay near his San Diego home in 1984.

Top left: Steve Ford got a playful hug on the L.A. set of the TV soap opera he was appearing in when he was not tending to his horses on his San Luis Obispo ranch, 1984.

Center left: Chip and Jeff Carter, who were living outside Washington, D.C., at the time, rode in a forklift, which happened to be on the Ellipse across the street from the White House, for this 1984 photo.

Bottom left: Maureen Reagan with her husband Dennis Revell sat with their poodle outside their home near Los Angeles, 1989.

Right: Patti Davis, the Reagans' daughter, played water games with her dog in the backyard of her home in Santa Monica, California, 1991.

This spread and following: When I arrived at Rancho del Cielo near Santa Barbara, California, in August 1983, to photograph Mrs. Reagan for a *Life* cover story, she had almost no makeup on. She appeared fresh and natural — she looked great, actually. She did not want any stylists or makeup artists fussing over her. I've never known a first lady — or a celebrity, for that matter — with such complete confidence in the way she looked.

Above and right: As the president was getting the horses ready, I got the feeling Mrs. Reagan wasn't all too keen on their daily ride. She agreed to ride with him, just to please him. Before riding, the president hammered in some fence posts. The canoe ride, however, was another matter; both of the Reagans seemed to get a kick out of a cruise around the pond.

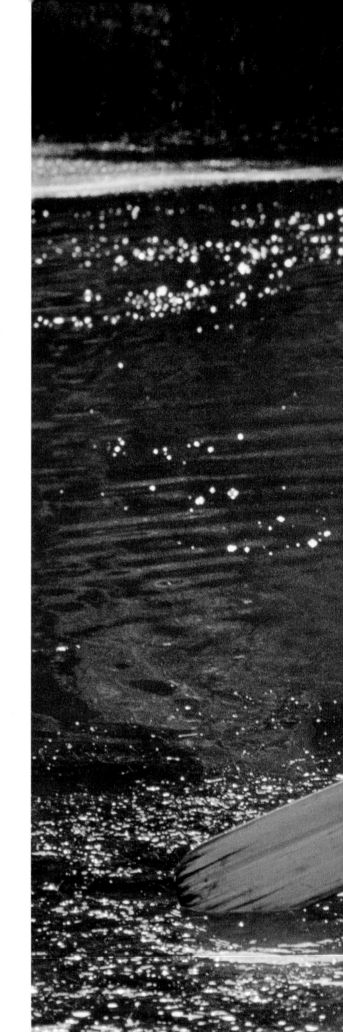

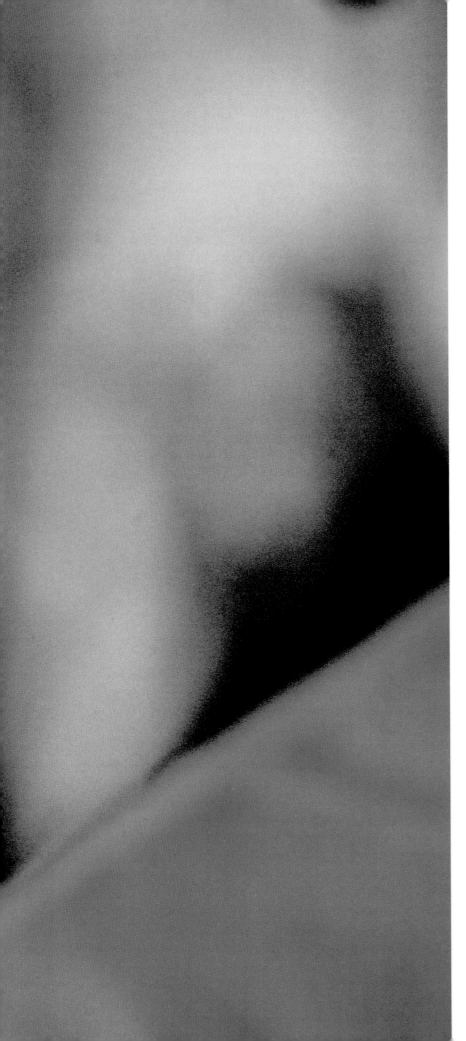

Left: In February 1968, Jacqueline Kennedy was on a ski holiday near Montreal. The day was bitter cold. A large crowd of skiers was waiting to go up on the lift when Jackie appeared, right in front of me. Basically, everyone was dressed alike. But you could spot Jackie a mile off, even with her face covered. You could see her eyes — there was no mistaking those eyes.

Above: In December 1967, Caroline, ten, romped with her dog in Manhattan's Central Park while her brother, John Jr., seven, hurled snowballs at a companion.

Left: John and Caroline Kennedy, then twenty-four and twenty-seven, sat on the lawn behind the JFK Library in Boston in 1984 for a *Life* cover story I photographed on all twenty-three living first-generation descendants of the presidents. Here were members of the most photographed family in American history and suddenly they were telling me, in a thoroughly convincing way, that they had never posed for a formal portrait before and would I mind telling them what to do and how to pose.

Top: It was St. Patrick's Day, 1968. Senator Robert Kennedy had just announced his candidacy for the presidency and was marching in the parade up Fifth Avenue. I saw Bobby look up and tip his head, and when I looked up as well, there were his sister-in-law, Jacqueline Kennedy, and her son, John Jr., cheering him along.

Left: The first time I photographed Amy Carter was in Plains, Georgia, in 1976 — during her father's run for the presidency — at the home of her grandmother, Miss Lillian. Amy, at age nine, was perfectly natural, attended public school, and seemed to avoid wearing shoes all the time. She was — and remains — a free spirit.

Top right: When I photographed her eight years later, for *Life,* in the backyard of the Carter family home in Plains, she was a high school senior, still barefoot and wearing blue jeans and, this time, she had brought along her Siamese cat, Misty Malarkey Ying Yang.

Bottom right: What was interesting about the Carters in general was that everything was so up front: "This is the way we are, take it or leave it." The president made no excuses for his brother, Billy, who was quite jovial and who really liked to have a good drink, or for his mother, a slightly eccentric sort who happened to be a volunteer in the Peace Corps. During a photo shoot in 1976, with son Billy looking on, Miss Lillian told me she was the "chief" of the family and had a headdress to prove it. Naturally, I took that as a cue for a photo.

Top left: George Bush, then a candidate for the presidency, got up very early for a pre-jog stretch during the 1988 New Hampshire primary.

Bottom left: Before he was tapped by President Reagan to be his running mate, George Bush sat with his wife, Barbara, by their Houston swimming pool, in March of 1978.

Right: That same day, Bush took a swim with his cocker spaniel, C. Fred.

Above: For a 1984 *Life* photo essay on the children of past presidents, Luci Baines Johnson Turpin walked through a replica of the Oval Office at the Johnson Library near the campus of the University of Texas at Austin. The entire series of portraits of presidents' children is now a part of the permanent collection of the National Portrait Gallery in Washington, D.C.

Left: In the East Room of the White House, LBJ's daughter Luci, with her son Patrick Nugent Jr., watched as her father welcomed astronauts Lovell, Anders, and Borman back to Earth, January 1969.

Above: In December 1992, a high-spirited Lady Bird Johnson blew out the candles at her eightieth birthday celebration in Austin while daughters Lynda Bird and Luci watched.

Right: Lynda Bird Johnson Robb, married to Virginia governor Chuck Robb, posed in the governor's mansion in 1984.

Above: Mrs. Nixon took her shoes off as she sat in the president's favorite chair on the second floor of the White House in this 1972 photo for *Life.* This was the chair her husband would settle into, to think over things, at the end of each day.

Left: David and Julie Nixon Eisenhower rode around Camp David, the presidential retreat, in a golf cart in 1972.

Above: President and Mrs. Nixon liked to have tea on the Truman Balcony, as this 1972 photograph showed.

Right: Julie Nixon Eisenhower sat at her desk in the rarely photographed third-floor private quarters of the White House, in September of 1972.

Right: At his San Clemente home in 1978, President Nixon beams at his first granddaughter, Jennie, as mother Julie Nixon Eisenhower looks on, with the president's brothers Edward (left) and Donald (center).

Top: Julie and David Eisenhower gathered in the kitchen of their Pennsylvania home for this 1986 photograph with their children, Melanie, two, Jennie, eight, and Alex, six.

Above: Tricia Nixon Cox sat for a portrait with her son, Christopher, in their New York City living room, August 1984.

Left and top right: In June 1992, I photographed the Clintons playing Hearts, a card game the president's mother, Virginia Kelly, had taught him as a child. It was obvious from the banter that was going back and forth among them that they played cards regularly. The game became quite serious at one point, and when Chelsea made a tactical error, they made it plain she was going to learn from her mistakes — they weren't about to let her off the hook.

Center right: Mrs. Clinton and daughter Chelsea, thirteen, had been riding their bicycles on the grounds of their Little Rock home when they stopped to rest. You could tell that it was dawning on them that no matter how busy their lives had been while Clinton was the governor of Arkansas, they were about to experience an even more hectic and heady lifestyle, December 1992.

Bottom right: Chelsea being kissed by her father outside the governor's mansion in Little Rock, Arkansas, in June 1992.

Left: In December 1992, after Bill Clinton was elected president, I photographed the family in Little Rock again, just prior to their move to the capital. This time the soon-to-be first couple stood in front of a portrait of Chelsea, depicted as an angel, that would serve as their Christmas card that year.

Above: Mrs. Virginia Kelly, Clinton's mother, hugged a portrait of her son at her home in Hot Springs, Arkansas, in late 1992. She was so proud and was having the time of her life. All of her girlfriends, who gathered once a week for lunch, were elated along with her.

POLITICS

Following a parade down Pennsylvania Avenue to celebrate the astronauts' safe return after having orbited the moon, President Lyndon Johnson hosted a ceremony in the East Room of the White House in January 1969. As crew members James Lovell and William Anders looked on, Frank Borman gave Johnson a photograph of Earth, taken from space, and remarked, "Mr. President, we'd like to present you with a photograph of the LBJ ranch in Texas." That got a big laugh.

Previous spread: In looking back over the photographs I had taken of the Reagans in New Hampshire on the 1976 campaign trail, I found this portrait of Mrs. Reagan eating a sandwich, alone, looking out the window of a moving bus. You see the desolate snow, mile after mile of bleak roads, telephone poles, nameless towns. And no guarantee of reaching your goal, despite all the sacrifices you have made in order to finally arrive where you want to be. This is the surreal life the candidates and their wives have to endure — a lot of sandwiches on buses — to get to the state dinners and balls at the White House.

Above: She was the toast of London and Paris when President and Mrs. Kennedy took Europe by storm in 1961. Crowds would shout, "Jackie, Jackie," which led the president to remark that he was the man who escorted Jackie Kennedy to Paris. President and Mrs. Kennedy are shown here as they leave a reception in London.

Left: It was an official state visit to France in 1961. And there, along the boulevard, came President Kennedy, with French president Charles de Gaulle at his side, horses galloping in front and behind them. This is what I've always thought an official state visit should look like: the procession, the crowds, the festive dress uniforms of the soldiers, the sense of pomp and circumstance.

Top: In December 1986, Vice President George Bush went to the Capitol Building for a swearing-in ceremony in the room that had served as the old Supreme Court. Very Victorian in style, with swags of red velvet behind the justices' seats, it was an interesting backdrop.

Left: At an important conference in Glassboro, New Jersey, in 1967 with Soviet Premier Aleksei Kosygin, President Lyndon Johnson was accompanied by his secretaries of defense and state, Robert McNamara and Dean Rusk. This was the first time LBJ had spoken to the Russians on his home turf. The meeting took place at the height of the Vietnam war, when tensions ran high between the superpowers. As the president emerged from the meeting, he came out with a wide grin. It was the first time I'd ever seen him smile.

Top: In this 1973 photograph, Gerald Ford had just been confirmed as vice president and the press descended upon him.

Right: President Richard Nixon and his running mate Spiro Agnew were joined on the podium in Miami at the 1972 Republican National Convention by Gerald Ford, the man who would later replace Agnew as vice president.

Right: While campaigning for reelection in 1972, President Nixon was way ahead of George McGovern in the polls and decided to ride in an open car down the streets of Laredo, Texas. Supporters cheered him along the route. I jumped out of the car ahead of him as he started to work the crowd, shaking hands. Because I'd been traveling with the campaign that year, the Secret Service agents knew who I was and allowed me to move in and out. Their eyes remained fixed on the sea of people around us.

Above: At a 1978 reception for Richard Nixon, given by his former White House staff, the president was reunited with Diane Sawyer. He asked her, "Have you still got that nice, long blond hair?" Smiling, she twirled to show him. Sawyer, an accomplished broadcast journalist today, had served in Nixon's White House press office and later at San Clemente.

Left: This East Room farewell in 1974 was one of the century's most important presidential moments. For the first time in history, an American president was resigning. I knew Mrs. Nixon was an emotional person, not as stiff as the press had made her out to be. During President Nixon's poignant speech to his staff on his last day in office, Mrs. Nixon stood strong and straight, but her eyes told the story.

Top right: In the spring of 1974, Mrs. Nixon seemed genuinely pleased as she entertained a delegation of Republican women from Virginia in the Blue Room. She had remarkable poise considering the fact that the Watergate investigation was in full swing. I remember White House correspondent Helen Thomas turning to me that day and commenting about the first lady's composure in the face of such difficulties. "Look at this woman," she whispered. "She's amazing, just amazing."

Center right: Nixon and Soviet leader Leonid Brezhnev chatted on a White House balcony in 1973. This intimate whisper, coaxed from a foe, was vintage Nixon. He was an extraordinary statesman and diplomat who could turn former enemies like Brezhnev and Sadat and Chou En-lai into confidants.

Bottom right: In 1978, President Nixon was coming back into the public eye and I joined him in Paris in his hotel room at the Ritz. I remember drawing his attention to the group of photographers standing in the street below. "You must always give them a little each day," he said. "Not too much, just a little. Because they've got a job to do." I've always thought the remark revealed a considerate sentiment. One night during that Paris trip, he invited me into his suite to talk. He was wearing an elegant dressing gown. I asked if I could photograph him and, embarrassed, he shook his head no. It was a shame because it would have shown a more informal side to his personality.

Right: No one had been allowed access to photograph President Carter aboard his plane, when I asked press secretary Jody Powell if I could get a lift back to New York. It was during that period in 1979 when the strain of rigorous campaigning was beginning to show. This picture gives a gritty, very real sense of the exhaustion and turmoil that were engulfing Carter at the time.

Top: Sequestered in his St. Louis hotel suite before a 1992 presidential debate with George Bush and Ross Perot, candidate Clinton sat alone, poring over his notes. He had the focused, determined look of a prizefighter before he enters the ring.

Bottom: George Bush working at his desk in the study of his Houston home in 1978.

THE
WHITE
HOUSE

Top left: Mrs. Clinton, in the Blue Room, held a tulip named for her by the government of the Netherlands in this 1994 photograph.

Bottom left: Mrs. Nixon posed for this *Life* cover on the second floor of the White House in 1972.

Right: In response to my having asked her where she did her work, Mrs. Carter brought me into the master bedroom, which had a desk in one corner, and said, "Right here." For this 1980 photo she sat at the end of her bed.

Previous spread: Pat Nixon boarded a helicopter on the White House lawn as she went about her duties as first lady, 1972.

Left: Leonid Brezhnev was in Washington, D.C., in 1973 for a state visit. As he headed for a dinner in his honor, the Soviet leader decided to play a joke on me, suddenly coming right up to the camera and breaking into a mischievous grin. His mood changed from somber to playful, just as he neared the lens. It was a spontaneous sequence that I never expected to get.

Right: At a cocktail reception in the Red Room, Nixon and Brezhnev were concentrating so intently on their discussion that they seemed oblivious to the other guests.

Previous spread: Mrs. Bush, accompanied by faithful Millie, posed in the Red Room in 1990. Mrs. Reagan wore a Galanos dress in the same setting, four years earlier.

Chef Henry Haller (left) and assistant chef Hans Rafferty sliced vegetables and stuffed 150 squabs in preparation for the state dinner honoring the British prime minister, Harold Wilson, in 1975.

Fourteen-foot-high weeping ficus trees were brought into the State Dining Room from the White House greenhouse for the evening.

The Grand Foyer was cleaned and polished in preparation for dancing.

Domestic red wine and champagne were carried into the dining room for after-dinner toasts.

American bird decoys were used as the centerpieces as a nod to Mr. Wilson, who was an amateur ornithologist.

Mrs. Ford entertained guests in the East Room before dinner.

Prime Minister Harold Wilson, President Gerald Ford, Mrs. Mary Wilson, and Mrs. Betty Ford enter the gold and white State Dining Room for dinner.

With Mrs. Wilson seated next to him, President Ford seemed pleased with the evening.

Actor Warren Beatty was among the mixture of political and entertainment luminaries. Carved on the fireplace are words by John Adams: "May none but Honest and Wise Men ever rule under This Roof."

Opera diva Beverly Sills sang after dinner next to a portrait of George Washington.

Margaret Truman Daniel, daughter of the thirty-third president of the United States, Harry Truman, with her husband, Clifton, danced to the Marine Combo Band.

The Honorable Elliot L. Richardson and Mrs. Richardson (center) danced among the many guests at the end of the festive evening.

Top right: It's hard to imagine, but there is a normal life going on behind the scenes in the private quarters on the second floor of the White House. I went to photograph the first lady in late 1979. The second story's half-oval windows in the West Sitting Hall are very photogenic, so as we went by one of them I asked Mrs. Carter to pick up her one-year-old grandchild, Sarah, daughter of Jack and Judy. The first lady agreed, and smiled. The windows were frosted over from the cold but the act of lifting up and hugging a grandchild gave the picture an added warmth.

Left: Mrs. Carter was helping Amy get ready for school upstairs in the White House in November 1979.

Center right: Later she brushed her daughter's hair as Amy did her homework. What is interesting about the photographs is that you see how different families use the White House so that they will not forget their time there.

Bottom right: The Carters were as natural as you would expect them to be in Plains, except for the fact that there were butlers in tails waiting on them while Amy studied at the breakfast table.

Top: Tricia Nixon and her fiancé, Ed Cox, sat in the back of a limousine on their way to a reception in 1971.

Above: Tricia, Julie, and Ed Cox's sister Maise had been out shopping for Tricia's upcoming wedding and stopped in front of the White House to unload the day's purchases.

Right: When I photographed Julie Nixon Eisenhower in her matron of honor's gown for sister Tricia's 1971 wedding, they posed in the Lincoln bedroom. It was said to have been Jacqueline Kennedy's favorite room in the White House, where she liked to sit and feel the presence of Abraham Lincoln. Sir Winston Churchill, in fact, after having spent a night there, publicly announced he had seen the ghost of Lincoln in the room — a legend that persists today. Both Julie and Tricia laughingly said they had glimpsed Lincoln's ghost as well.

Here are four views of the White House Oval Office.

Above: I caught President Carter working alone in 1979.

Left: President Nixon's image was reflected in his desk, 1974.

Above: President Clinton in an exuberant gesture caught a
football thrown by chief of staff Mac McLarty in 1993.

Right: President Ford met with his secretary of state,
Henry Kissinger, 1975.

PRIVATE
LIVES

Right: President Jimmy Carter has always exemplified the ethic of hard work. In 1995, at his home in Plains, Georgia, I photographed him for *Life* cleaning his backyard tennis court. Imagine a president washing down his own tennis court. It's that religious ethic from his youth: work, work, work. He stays very fit and focuses on each project, one at a time, to accomplish his goals.

Above: I traveled with the Carters to Africa in 1995 on a world health fact-finding mission. They seemed to do almost everything together, even reading quietly on the long plane ride home.

Previous spread: President Carter went fishing in the pond at his boyhood home in Plains, Georgia, 1995.

Lady Bird Johnson stood overlooking the pastureland on the LBJ ranch in Johnson City, Texas, in 1985. It stretched for as far as you could see and was actually very flat, like most of the Texas land I have seen. We saw some purple gayfeathers, and I asked her to sit among them, even though they were not Texas bluebonnets, the state flower that she had worked to plant by every highway in the state. The president and Lady Bird had retired to the ranch after his term of office where Mrs. Johnson continued to work on the beautification program for America.

Top right: Susan Ford Vance played with her children, Tyne, four, and Heather, nearly two, in 1984 on the deck of their suburban Virginia home. Susan had the distinction of having her senior prom on the White House lawn and later worked as a photographer before marrying former Secret Service agent Charles Vance.

Left: At their summer home near Aspen, Colorado, Mrs. Ford worked on plans for the expansion of the Betty Ford Center while the president kept her company, 1984.

Bottom right: Mrs. Ford sat poolside at home in Rancho Mirage near Palm Springs, California, 1979.

It was a beautiful summer day, bright and sunny, when I arrived at President Ford's home near Aspen, Colorado, in August 1987. I had come to photograph him for a *Life* article on former presidents. I was happy to see that his granddaughters Tyne, seven, and Heather, four, daughters of Susan Ford Vance, were visiting at the time. I asked if they would go outside to the field behind the house for a photograph. They did, and picked a few flowers for their grandfather. The president smiled with pride.

Above: In January 1978, while in California to photograph President Nixon upon publication of his new book, I mentioned to him that I had been all over the world with him but had never been to his boyhood home in Yorba Linda, which has since become part of the Richard Nixon Presidential Library and Birthplace. He was happy to pose outside, inside — even sitting down for a photograph on the bed he'd slept in as a boy. "This is a good old house, isn't it?" he asked me, looking around wistfully.

Right: Richard Nixon was living in his San Clemente home, Casa Pacifica, when this portrait was taken in 1978. It was just at sunset and the president asked me to accompany him on a stroll around the grounds, overlooking the Pacific Ocean. He told me that early evening was his favorite time of day and that this was his favorite spot. "I often come here to sit and look out at the ocean," he said, as the day's final rays of sunlight fell behind the trees.

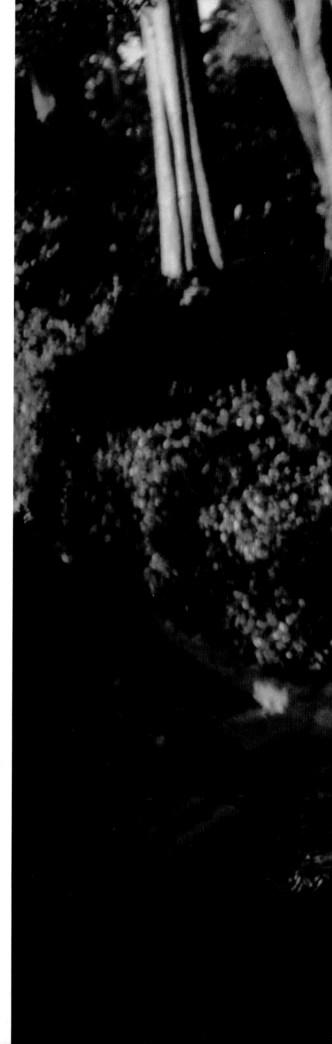

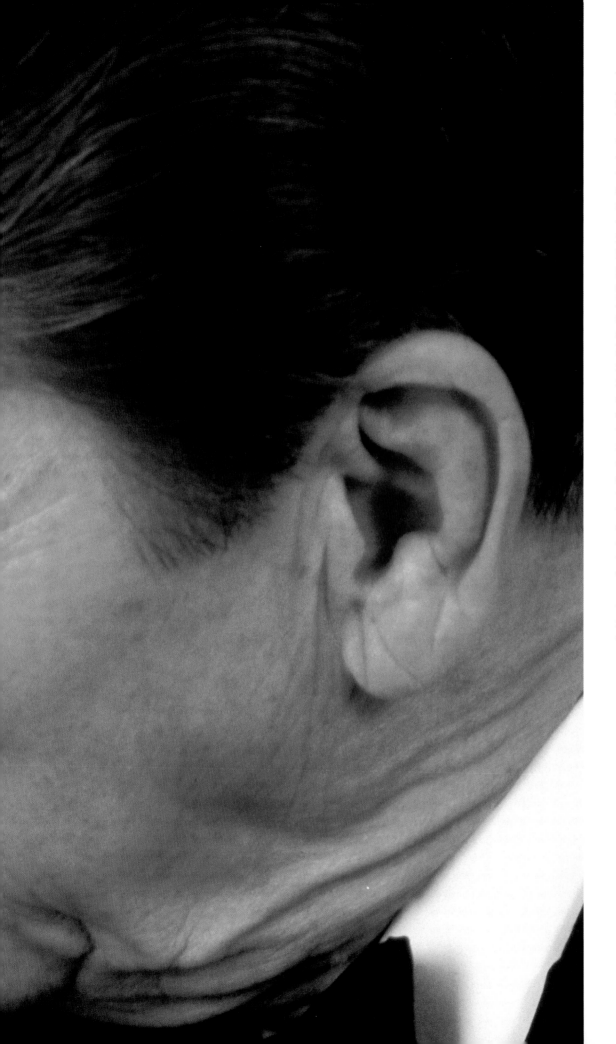

When *Vanity Fair* asked me to photograph President and Mrs. Reagan for a cover story in 1985, I knew they would give us only a short time. As it turned out, they stopped by on their way to a state dinner and stayed exactly six minutes. Before they arrived, a backdrop of white no-seam paper was set up in a small room off the main ballroom, and as they entered, I put on a tape of Frank Sinatra singing "Nancy (With the Laughing Face)." That brought smiles to their faces, and they started dancing. Their aides hadn't expected all of this — in fact, they would have turned me down had I mentioned the concept beforehand — but once the thing was set in motion, they were afraid to interrupt. In addition to a series of dancing photos, I had envisioned a kiss as a finishing touch, since it was apparent that theirs was a genuine love story. So I had a camera with a close-up lens ready. I asked them to kiss. And they did so, willingly. I had in mind a great 1940s Hollywood fadeout, like the ones at the end of all those movies I'd seen as a boy in Glasgow.

Left: With the Kennedys' Cape Cod home as a backdrop, Caroline Bouvier Kennedy hugged her uncle, Senator Edward Kennedy, who had escorted her down the aisle that afternoon to wed Edwin Schlossberg at Our Lady of Victory church in Hyannis Port on July 19, 1986.

Top right: The bride and groom seemed relaxed after the ceremony as they stood on the beach where Caroline played as a child.

Below: Bridesmaids from left: Sydney Lawford McKelvy, Nicole Lefton, Courtney Kennedy Ruhe, Susan Minot, Nicole Seligman, Caroline Minot, Julie Agoos, and matron of honor Maria Shriver. Flower girls: Clara and Analise Rosenthal.

Following spread: Caroline Kennedy, with usher William Ivey and cousin Tina Radziwill, smiled for what would become a *Life* cover. The day was beautiful, and Caroline was making the most of it, even though her mother had been nervous in the church. Of all the photographs I took that day, Caroline, her mother, and I all agreed that this was the one we liked best.